# THE S
## AND CHIPS
## JOKE BOOK

C000137414

Also available by Scoular Anderson:

**MY FIRST JOKE BOOK**
**A – Z OF ANIMAL JOKES**

Published by Young Corgi Books

# THE SPIDER AND CHIPS JOKE BOOK

## SCOULAR ANDERSON

YOUNG CORGI BOOKS

THE SPIDER AND CHIPS JOKE BOOK

A YOUNG CORGI BOOK   0 552 525308

Originally published in Great Britain by Young Corgi Books

PRINTING HISTORY
Young Corgi edition published 1989

Text and illustrations copyright © Scoular Anderson, 1989

*Conditions of sale*
1.  This book is sold subject to the condition that it shall not, by way of trade *or otherwise*, be lent, re-sold, hired out or otherwise circulated in any form of binding or cover other than that in which it is published *and without a similar condition including this condition being imposed on the subsequent purchaser.*
2.  This book is sold subject to the Standard Conditions of Sale of Net Books and may not be re-sold in the UK below the net price fixed by the publishers for the book.

This book is set in 14/16pt Baskerville

Young Corgi Books are published by Transworld Publishers Ltd., 61–63 Uxbridge Road, Ealing, London W5 5SA, in Australia by Transworld Publishers (Australia) Pty. Ltd., 15–23 Helles Avenue, Moorebank, NSW 2170, and in New Zealand by Transworld Publishers (N.Z.) Ltd., Cnr. Moselle and Waipareira Avenues, Henderson, Auckland.

Made and printed in Great Britain by
The Guernsey Press Co Ltd., Guernsey, Channel Islands

To the Brown family

**Knock knock.**
Who's there?
**Cook.**
Cook who?
**That's the first one I've heard this year!**

11

What's a vampire's favourite soup?
**Scream of tomato.**

What's the fly doing in the alphabet
soup?
**Learning to read.**

13

15

# A BREATHTAKING BREAKFAST

Tommy rushes to the table,
Pulls a chair up to his place.
Hunger pangs inside his stomach
Make him rush at headlong pace.

'Try this new, exciting cereal!'
says the wording on the packet.
'Snap and crackle will be nothing
When you've heard this modern racket!'

Tommy carefully pours the milk on,
Ready for the slightest sound.
What he hears near blows his specs off,
Makes the very house resound.

'WHAMADAM!' his breakfast utters,
Amplified as heavy rock.
Bits of cereal flying skywards
Make the budgie faint with shock.

'WHAMADAMA-RAMADAMA!'
Makes the knives and spoons go clatter.
Tommy grips the table tightly,
Plates and cups and saucers shatter.

When the noise at last grows quieter,
Tommy, weak and slightly reeling,
Steps with care upon a chair
And scrapes his breakfast off the
  ceiling.

# EXCITING EGGS

**Knock knock.**
Who's there?
**Egbert.**
Egbert who?
**Egbert no bacon.**

What's yellow and soft and goes round
and round?
**A long-playing omelette.**

Why are eggs like bricks?
**They have to be laid.**

**Did you hear the one about the three eggs?**
No.
**Two bad.**

Where do tough chickens come from?
**Hard-boiled eggs.**

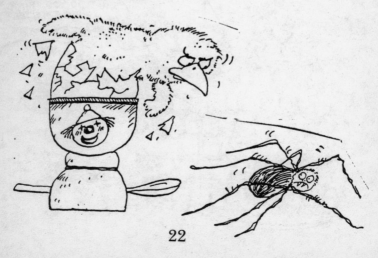

What kind of motorbike can cook eggs?
**A scrambler.**

# BOTHERSOME BITES

The onion's a sad one I fear,
For whenever you draw close to hear,
The tale it can tell
Will make your heart swell
And undoubtedly bring forth a tear.

In order to conquer her pasta,
Patricia ate fasta and fasta,
But all that she got
Was a gigantic knot
And her lunch was a tangled disasta.

The orange has a leathery skin
And it's awkward to find a way in,
For the bad-tempered fruit
Will probably shoot
A shower of juice at your chin.

26

Said a girl in a bad-tempered state:
'Holes in cheese are something I *hate*!'
Said her mum: 'If you please,
You can just eat the cheese.
Leave the holes on the side of your
    plate.'

Garlic is nasty to chew,
But something that's worthwhile to do,
For the smell of your breath
Will put vampires to death —
Though it drives all your friends away
    too.

If you think you have chewed quite
  enough
On caramel or gum that is tough,
Don't tuck it away
To continue next day —
You'll find it all covered in fluff.

# FRUIT AND VEG

What's green and sings?
**Elvis Parsley.**

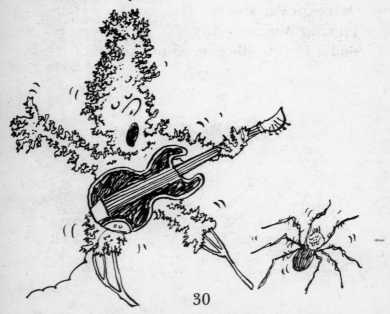

31

**Knock knock.**
Who's there?
**Lettuce.**
Lettuce who?
**Lettuce in and you'll find out.**

What do geese eat?
**Gooseberries.**

What's short, green and goes camping?
**A boy sprout.**

What did one strawberry say to the other strawberry?
**We shouldn't be in this jam.**

What did the hedgehog have for lunch?
**Prickled onions.**

35

What vegetable needs a plumber?
**A leek.**

What should you do if you swallow a
plum stone?
**Call a plumber.**

Why should you never tell jokes in a greengrocer's?
**Because potatoes have eyes and beanstalk.**

39

What's the difference between a mouldy
lettuce and a dismal song?
**One's a bad salad and the other's a sad
ballad.**

**Knock knock.**
Who's there?
**Banana.**
Banana who?
**Knock knock.**
Who's there?
**Banana.**
Banana who?
**Knock knock.**
Who's there?
**Banana.**
Banana who?
**Knock knock.**
Who's there?
**Orange.**
Orange who?
**Orange glad I didn't say banana?**

Why did the apple turnover?
**Because it saw the swiss roll.**

What's yellow and goes click?
**A ball-point banana.**

43

Where had the runner bean?
**To see the celery stalk.**

What's purple and hums?
**An electric plum.**

Why did the oranges run into the middle
of the road?
**They wanted to play squash.**

Why did the orange go to the doctor?
**Because he wasn't peeling well.**

Why did the tomato run?
**To ketchup.**

**Knock knock.**
Who's there?
**Pear.**
Pear who?
**Pear of shoes.**

**Knock knock.**
Who's there?
**Shoes.**
Shoes who?
**Shoes me, I didn't mean to step on your pear.**

48

49

The haggis is a fancy thing
With round and shining skin;
Its ends are tied with knotted string
Or skewered with a pin.

Some say the haggis is a bird,
For surely it has wings,
And in the evening it is heard
As charmingly it sings.

Yet others say the haggis grows
On giant forest trees;
Like fruit the haggis hang in rows
And may be plucked with ease.

The haggis is an egg, it's said,
By those who seem to know;
Across the moors these eggs are spread
By some gargantuan crow.

But Scots, who know the haggis well,
Regard it as a meal;
They savour its delicious smell
While bagpipes rant and squeal.

But wait . . . A skilful chef named Pete,
While holidaying on Mull,
Discovered that this haggis meat
Was really rather dull.

He had a picture in his head
Of haggis filled with spice,
Served upon a tasty bed
Of saffron-flavoured rice.

And so on unsuspecting folk
Pete offered with a flurry,
A dish that made them gasp and choke —
A fiery haggis curry.

53

# MEAT MIXTURE

What do ghosts eat for supper?
**Ghoulash.**

What's the best thing to put in a pie?
**Your teeth.**

WAITER, WAITER, THERE'S A WORM ON MY PLATE!

NO SIR, THAT'S THE SAUSAGE

What happened when the cow jumped
over the moon?
**The price of beef went up.**

What kind of thief steals meat?
**A hamburglar.**

What happened when there was a fight in the fish and chip shop?
**A lot of fish got battered.**

# SOMETHING SWEET

How can you tell when there's an elephant in your custard?
**By the lumps.**

What's wrong with a man with jelly in one ear and sponge-cake in the other? **He's a trifle deaf.**

What sort of meringue always comes back?
**A boomeringue.**

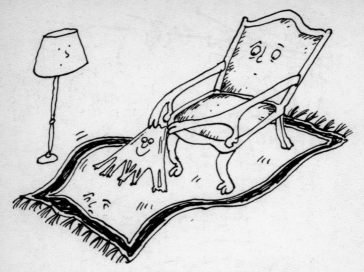

What did the bubblegum say to the carpet?
**I'm stuck on you.**

How do you start a pudding race?
**Sago.**

What's a frog's favourite sweet?
**A lollihop.**

**Knock knock.**
Who's there?
**Alick.**
Alick who?
**Alick my lollipop.**

**Knock knock.**
Who's there?
**Felix.**
Felix who?
**Felix my lollipop, I'll lick his.**

Why did the jelly wobble?
**Because it saw the milk shake.**

What pudding is unfit?
**The apple puff.**

What's yellow and stupid?
**Thick custard.**

What pudding is bad-tempered?
**Apple grumble.**

Slowly Susan sieves the sugar
From the silver sugar-shaker.
Simply sifting lumpish sugar
Ensures the sugar sprinkles sweetly.

72

Famished Freddie fried fresh fish,
Fine flat fillets filled with flavour,
But the fish flapped fattish fins
And flew into the flickering fire.

# DISASTROUS DRINKS

Why do magicians drink lots of tea?
**Because sorcerers need cuppas.**

75

What's a frog's favourite drink?
**Croaka-Cola.**

# AFTERNOON TEA WITH AUNTY

My dear, how nice to see you!
My dear, do please step in!
Take off your coat and scarf, dear,
My dear, you do look thin!

Here's a cup of tea, dear.
What would you like to eat?
You can be sure at Aunty's
You're bound to find a treat.

Put more jam on the scone, dear,
More butter on the bread.
Spread syrup on the crumpets,
Would you rather have treacle instead?

The muffins are only half-heated,
But don't be half-hearted with these.
Take a handful to keep yourself going,
Take some more whenever you please!

Here's honey to put on the toast, dear,
And all sorts of fancy preserves.
A sweet little niece like you, dear,
Gets all the delights she deserves.

There's a tart and a flan and a pie,
    dear,
There's even chocolate gateau.
Put some cream all over the gingerbread,
Come, dear, don't be slow!

But you look a little pale, dear,
Is there enough fresh air?
What are you doing down there, dear?
You've broken my favourite chair!

Shall I tell you the joke about the butter?
**I'd better not, you'd only spread it!**

Two biscuits were walking down the road.
One got run over.
What did the other one say?

What do pixies have for tea?
**Fairy-cakes.**

Why did the girl put milk and sugar on the television set?
**She was watching a cereal.**

**Knock knock.**
Who's there?
**Arthur.**
Arthur who?
**Arthur any biscuits left?**

When do astronauts eat?
**At launch time.**

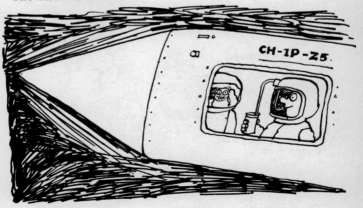

CH-1P-25.

Why did the girl keep a loaf of bread
in her comic?
**Because she liked crummy jokes.**

What kind of crisps are named after an
Arab ruler?
**Sultan vinegar.**

What cake gives you an electric shock?
**A currant bun.**

What do you do if someone offers you a plate of rock-cakes?
**Take your pick.**

What's the difference between an
elephant and a biscuit?
**Have you ever tried dunking an
elephant in your tea?**

What did the biscuit say to the almond?
**You're nuts and we're crackers!**

# AN ODD PEAR

JIB & SPROCKITT

*DELICIOUS FOODS*

Mr Jib and Mr Sprockitt
Admire their latest line in food.
A crunchy pear in luscious syrup
Looks enticing, tastes so good!

'But,' says Jib, 'the colour's dullsome!'
So Sprockitt adds some special dye.
Now the pear is fairly dazzling,
The juice is sparkling to the eye.

'It seems the dye has dimmed the
    flavour,'
Mr Sprockitt now points out.
Says Jib, 'A little extra sweetener
Will do the trick without a doubt.'

'And now I'll add this secret liquid —
Keeps fruit fresh for several years!'
But both men give a worried gasp —
The pear turns blue then disappears.

They add some this, they add some that,
They strain the liquid through a sack.
At last to their immense relief,
The pear, though purple, does come
   back.

'This frightful fruit will never sell!'
Says Sprockitt with a downcast air.
Says Jib, 'Just watch the shoppers rush
For Jib and Sprockitt's Purple Pear!'

They sup the mixture one more time,
Agree it is beyond compare,
Though neither sees that from his ears
Are growing tufts of purple hair.

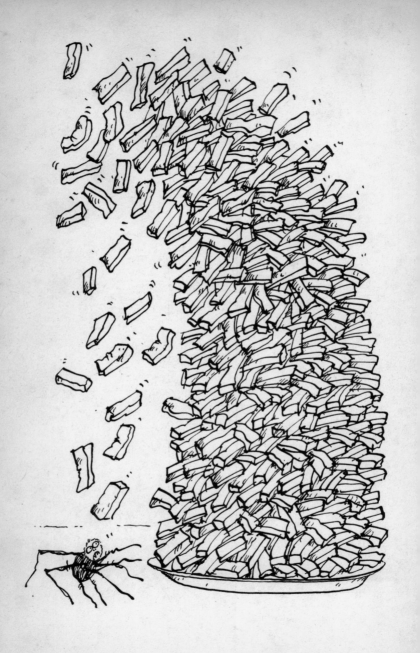